Living and Nonliving in the Mountains

Mountains

Rebecca Rissman

Heinemann LIBRARY
Chicago, Illinois

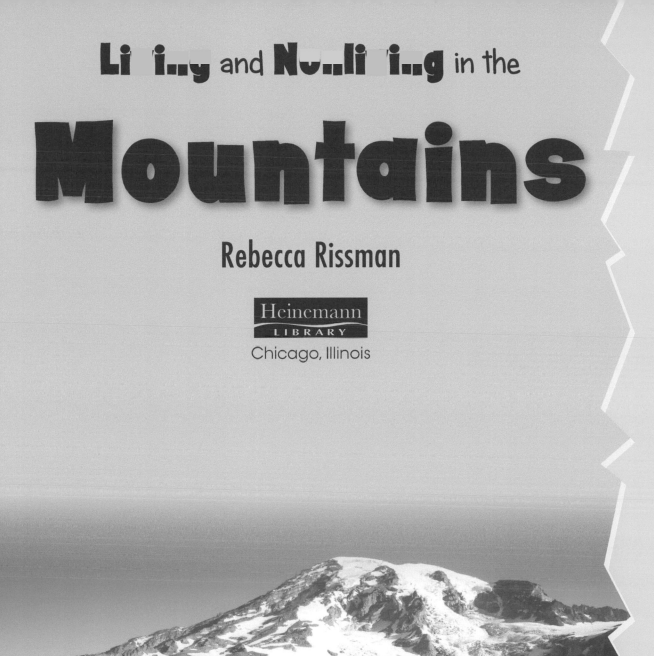

© 2014 Heinemann Library
an imprint of Capstone Global Library, LLC
Chicago, Illinois

To contact Capstone Global Library please phone
800-747-4992, or visit our website
www.capstonepub.com

Edited by Daniel Nunn, Rebecca Rissman, and
Catherine Veitch
Designed by Cynthia Della-Rovere
Picture research by Tracy Cummins
Production by Sophia Argyris
Originated by Capstone Global Library Ltd

ISBN 978-1-4109-5385-8 (hc)
ISBN 978-1-4109-5392-6 (pb)

Library of Congress Cataloging-in-Publication Data

Rissman, Rebecca.
  Living and nonliving in the mountains / Rebecca Rissman.
      pages cm.—(Is it living or nonliving?)
  Includes bibliographical references and index.
  ISBN 978-1-4109-5385-8 (hb)—ISBN 978-1-4109-
5392-6 (pb) 1. Mountains—Juvenile literature. 2. Life
(Biology)—Juvenile literature. I. Title.

  QH87.R57 2013
  577.5'3—dc23

Acknowledgments
We would like to thank the following for permission
to reproduce photographs:Getty Images pp. 14 (©
Joseph Van Os), 18 (© Klaus Nigge); Shutterstock pp.
1, 21 (© Christopher Boswell), 4, 23a (© Rigucci), 5 (©
Standa Riha), 6 (© Eduard Kyslynskyy), 7 (© Ekaterina
Pokrovsky), 8, 23d (© Galyna Andrushko), 9, 23c (© Jiri
Vavricka), 10 (© Popova Valeriya), 11, 23b (© μ), 12 (©
Paul Aniszewski), 13 (© Sergey Toronto), 15 (© Dennis
Donohue), 16 (© SergeyIT), 17 (© Joel Whitaker), 19
(© Wendy Nero), 20 (© Asaf Eliason), 21(©Christopher
Boswell), 22 (© pixy).

Front cover photograph of a mountain goat with kid in Utah
reproduced with permission of Superstock (© Animals
Animals).

We would like to thank Michael Bright and Nancy Harris for
their invaluable help in the preparation of this book.

Every effort has been made to contact copyright holders
of material reproduced in this book. Any omissions will be
rectified in subsequent printings if notice is given to the
publisher.

All the Internet addresses (URLs) given in this book were
valid at the time of going to press. However, due to the
dynamic nature of the Internet, some addresses may
have changed, or sites may have changed or ceased to
exist since publication. While the author and publisher
regret any inconvenience this may cause readers, no
responsibility for any such changes can be accepted by
either the author or the publisher.

Some words are in bold, **like this**.
You can find them in the glossary on page 23.

Contents

What Is a Mountain?

A mountain is a rocky, tall **landform**.

Mountains are very large.

4

Different types of plants and animals live on the mountains.

There are **nonliving** things in the mountains too.

What Are Living Things?

Living things are alive. Living things need air and **sunlight**.
Living things need food and water.

Living things grow and change.

Living things move on their own.

What Are Nonliving Things?

Nonliving things are not alive. Nonliving things do not need air and **sunlight**.

Nonliving things do not need food or water.

Nonliving things do not grow and change on their own.

Nonliving things do not move on their own.

Is a Pine Tree Living or Nonliving?

A pine tree needs water.

A pine tree moves on its own toward the sun.

A pine tree grows and changes.

A pine tree needs air and **sunlight**.

A pine tree is **living**.

Is Ice Living or Nonliving?

Ice does not move on its own.

Ice does not grow.

Ice does not need food.

Ice does not need air or **sunlight**.

Icc is **nonliving**.

Is a Mountain Lion Living or Nonliving?

A mountain lion grows and changes.

A mountain lion needs food and water.

A mountain lion moves on its own.

A mountain lion needs air and **sunlight**.

A mountain lion is **living**.

Is Soil Living or Nonliving?

Soil does not move on its own.

Soil does not need food or water.

Soil does not grow on its own.

Soil does not need air or **sunlight**.

Soil is **nonliving**.

Is an Eagle Living or Nonliving?

An eagle grows and changes.

An eagle needs food and water.

An eagle moves on its own.

An eagle needs air and **sunlight**.

An eagle is **living**.

Is a Wildflower Living or Nonliving?

A wildflower moves on its own toward the sun.

A wildflower needs water.

A wildflower grows and changes.

A wildflower needs air and **sunlight**.

A wildflower is **living**.

What Do You Think?

Is this rock **living** or **nonliving**?

Glossary

landform natural shape in the land

living alive. Living things need food and water. They breathe and move on their own. They grow and change.

nonliving not alive. Nonliving things do not need food and water. They do not move on their own. They do not grow and change on their own.

sunlight light from the sun

Find Out More

Websites

Facthound offers a safe, fun way to find Internet sites related to this book. All of the sites on Facthound have been researched by our staff.

Here's all you do:
Visit www.facthound.com

Type in this code: 9781410953858

Books

Dickmann, Nancy. *Mount Everest (Explorer Tales)*. Chicago: Raintree, 2013.

Lindeen, Carol K. *Living and Nonliving*. Mankato, Minn.: Capstone, 2008.

Waldron, Melanie. *Mountains (Habitat Survival)*. Chicago: Raintree, 2013.

Index